I0463104

Salarytopia

Entry-level to Six Figures in 5 years;
An Insider's Guide

By Anderson Rand

Preface

You can make six figures in 5 years.

$100,000 + .

No, this isn't a Boiler Room, Ben Affleck speech moment. No, I don't guarantee it. But I guarantee the techniques in this book will make it possible to a dedicated person who makes intelligent decisions and is willing to work hard and sacrifice. I call it Salarytopia. If you were born after around 1985 or so, I have news for you. Most of the generations before you aren't impressed. In the business world, lots of them refer to you as the entitled generation. For some reason, your generation all seem to think that they are owed the job they got, and they should be richly rewarded for showing up, complaining and asking HR to buy them a new ergonomic chair. Well, good news. Everyone else acting that way makes it easier for *you* to stand out! You will get ahead. Dedicate yourself and follow the advice in this book, and it will happen.

Introduction

The economy may suck right now. If you are the prototypical person reading this book, you are somewhere near your college graduation, or maybe are entering the job market without a degree. You may have a job but are trying to find your way. Maybe that isn't quite your situation, but it is something like this:

You hope or expect to be starting a job soon, or recently did. You are somewhere near the definition of "entry-level". If you are astute, you know this is not where you want to end up. But it is where you start. Hence the term – entry-level.

Well, I am here to tell you the keys to taking that entry-level job and turning it into a true money maker in as short a time as possible. Follow these guidelines, and you can be earning six figures in just a few years. I did it, and I know others that have done it too. Beyond that, I've hired people and moved them through the ranks. I've talked to many other managers who have done the same. This works, and I know of countless examples.

This is real advice, from someone who has done it and

has shepherded people through it. It is not a get rich quick plan. This book is a quick read, concise and to the point. You don't need another textbook at this stage. But you are probably a little long on academics, and short on practical advice. This book will give you real tools to reach Salarytopia. It is not easy. But it is straightforward.

Most likely, you have friends that fall into a few categories.

- The spoiled kid who will get money from his mom or dad and his job won't really matter.
- The guy who has the cool job that everyone is jealous of. This only lasts for about 1-2 years. This is the guy who is a promoter at a club, or the beer distributor to all the bars in your area. Or maybe he is a lifeguard, spending his day on the beach. The coolness of these jobs ends quickly.
- The friend who somehow hit the entrepreneurial lottery and made a ton of money. This doesn't happen often, but good for them.
- The girl who interned at the same place every summer and has a job waiting for her. (She probably used a lot of these techniques, and trust me, she is in a good place.)
- Most commonly - The ones who all got hired

by the company that hires everybody. They recruit on your campus with the hard sell. Not a bad thing, but this book will be good advice for them. These can be great opportunities, but they need to be taken advantage of.

Chapter 1: Selecting a Job

This is an important step and can't be overlooked. Look for long term potential, not the big payday today. Don't make the decision based on how easy the job sounds. Consider the soundness of the company.

Johnny Short is graduating, and his uncle owns a storage facility. He offers him $50,000 a year to manage the night shift. Even better, Johnny will get to work with his younger cousin Tommy quite a bit when he comes in each morning. There isn't much to do, and Johnny can even play video games while he is there at night.

This kind of thing probably sounds pretty good to a guy like Johnny. And it's a great opportunity that a lot of smart people would quickly jump at. But let's review a few of the pitfalls.

1. His uncle wants to hire him for a lot of money, without any experience. How well managed is this firm?
2. Will this $50,000 paycheck go anywhere in 2-3 years? My money says no.
3. His younger cousin is also working there. If Johnny's uncle will hire Johnny with no

experience, cousin Tommy is probably in line for executive management. Meaning a) no path for Johnny and b) a less than optimal outlook for the company.

Another guy you know, Jake, is considering a job at a hospital, doing data entry for $30,000. The hospital is growing, and needs people to help with capturing patient data, especially since they recently took over the administrative work for 2 other hospitals in their network.

Sure doesn't sound exciting, and that work is probably not too much fun. I'll bet his days will be pretty long. But, to me, this sounds like a good opportunity. With the help of this book, Jake will be a team lead before he knows it, and a manager shortly thereafter. The data entry is just a stepping stone to prove yourself.

The health care industry is thriving. This hospital seems to be expanding and investing in technology, and it is a part of a bigger network of hospitals. They are working on automation but need staff to help with capacity. This will likely offer lots of opportunities for an intelligent person to get noticed while helping to improve things, and lots of opportunities to better themselves.

This topic could be another book all unto itself, but the key points are this:

- Think long-term about the company's prospects.
- Don't be put off by the nature of the work. With the techniques in this book, the job you get won't be the one you do for long.
- Consider the industry, and the income potential.
- Often there are tradeoffs between what sounds good now and where it can lead in the future.

Chapter 2: Starting your new job

So, you followed my advice on accepting a job. You turned down the job at the wine bar and accepted the one at the bank doing online customer service. Congratulations. I think you made the right call.

Now, you may be making $28,000 today, but you'll be making $128,000 in 6 years. And here is where I tell you how. These three things won't do it alone, and it won't be easy, but it can be done. You'll need to work hard and fore-go a lot of the social events you may be used to. You may even have to (gasp) work weekends. Your friends may be working 9-5 and playing basketball after work. They will probably tell you that you are crazy for working such long hours. They will also be jealous of your job in 3 years.

To maximize your impact, and to set yourself up for rapid advancement, you need to focus on four main areas (I call them pillars), for success. Now, some have more meat than others, but to succeed quickly in many organizations, you will likely need some window dressing as well.

The four pillars are these:

- Improve Yourself
- Market Yourself
- Forget Yourself
- Check Yourself

Improve Yourself – this is the real meat of the process. The idea is constantly trying to make yourself better – which is a benefit to you and your organization. Learning, practicing, expanding your skills and scope are key points here. If you work in a perfect corporation, this may be all that is needed. But most corporations are highly inefficient, and talent, knowledge, production and potential are not immediately recognized or rewarded.

Market Yourself – As I mentioned, most companies are far from perfect, and often that is based on managers who are not actively monitoring talent (you!). You may be the perfect employee and doing the job of someone 3 levels above you. That may not be noticed. Which is why you need to make sure that it is noticed. For me, this is the most difficult and frustrating part. I want to quietly do perfect work and leave it at that. I don't want to immodestly promote myself. I'll show you some techniques to market yourself without shameless self-promotion.

Forget Yourself – This one is vitally important. For you, your job is about you. For your company, it's about the process and about everyone in the company. You need to detach your actions and your viewpoints from just your perspective. You need to be a "team player". A lot of people consider this term a cliché, but whatever you call it, you can't advance rapidly without the other people in your organization, and outside it.

Check Yourself – This may be the most difficult to understand, and it is focused on those of you in the "Entitled Generation". You need to understand that having a job is not an inalienable right. It is not self-evident. It is a privilege, and you need to treat it that way. If you think things like "They can't do that." or "I'm going to sue them." on a frequent basis, you need to either change your attitude, or at least figure out how to fake it. They *can* fire you, and they *can* easily replace you if needed. And you *can't* sue them over it. To Check Yourself, you need to understand that you aren't doing the company a favor by working late, they are paying you for it, and they are letting you keep your job.

Chapter 3: Your First Day

Your first day will be a quick version of everything else. The four pillars will also apply, but on a smaller scale. Get a good night's sleep, dress more formally than required, show up early and with an eager attitude. Focus on learning names and the way around the building, and once you start actual work, have a notebook ready and take notes. Ask questions – the person training you may or may not know the answers, so if you don't get a strong answer, write it down for clarification later.

You will also get a lot of questions about you, so have an elevator speech ready. If they ask where you worked last, be prepared to say, "I actually just graduated from UCLA, so this is my first professional job. But I interned at Bank of California for two years." This is your first chance to market yourself (honestly), so be ready. And be ready to repeat it.

You will also be pretty much useless on your own at this point, so it's a great opportunity to practice that team-player attitude. A lot of places will have you twiddling your thumbs at some point during the day. Ask your new team mates if there is anything you can do to help them out, even something menial like filing papers or ticking things on a checklist.

And finally, remember the final pillar – check yourself. Your team or your manager may tell you that you need to wait until 1pm for lunch, or they may even ask you to (gasp) go get some coffee. You may be thinking, "They can't do that.". Forget it. Shut your mouth. Get them some coffee.

Chapter 4: Improve Yourself

Now, I have laid out the broad strokes of this concept earlier in the book, so now let me get into practical application. To use a sports analogy, this is the pro football player actually working to play better. This is studying playbooks, hitting the gym and practicing. Now, an NFL player requires a lot of talent. Luckily, talent is a much less important factor in corporate America.

Learn the bigger picture

You will probably have a few different people training you in your first few weeks. Some of them may "get it" and others may not. Try to spend as much time as possible with the ones that do.

As an example, your job may be to take inbound customer service calls. Your trainer may immediately launch into what responses to give if a customer is unhappy, and what button to press when they ask for a manager. But wait a second, back up. Who are these customers, why are they calling, where did they get this number? Are we trying to make them happy or answer questions, or give refunds?

Your better trainers will start with this kind of information and will focus on the bigger picture first. The guy who doesn't get it will not explain it, because he probably doesn't get it at all himself! He'll show you how to pull the arm of the machine but can't tell you what you are making.

You need to aggressively get the time with the guy who gets it. You won't be able to spend all of your time with him (remember – forget yourself – team-player), but you can certainly ask if you can spend mornings with him, and mention to your supervisor or manager that he seems to be the most effective at training you.

Constantly be learning
In the beginning, everything is new, so learning opportunities will be plentiful. But later on, it won't be so obvious. But it will still be available.

The idea is to understand the company in the same way that your senior managers do. Create a diagram in your head of how your department works, and how it interfaces with other teams and external parties. (It doesn't have to stay in your brain, draw it out on paper if it helps!)

Ask yourself, do I know everything there is to know about what I am doing? What was the last thing that I needed to ask a manager about? What does Bob across the aisle do? Seems different than my job. What does the "transitions" team on the other side of the room do? Those guys in "Technology Escalation" seem to be busy, but with what?

These are all things that you should ask about. Tell your manager you are interested in learning more about "X", and wonder if there may be an opportunity to do that? There should be. Maybe not right away, but a half-decent manager will aggressively embrace the fact that you want to learn. The more you start to learn more about, the more complete the flow-chart in your brain will be.

I've been in my industry for more than a decade, and I haven't come close to learning everything. There is always more to learn, and you need to keep a curious mindset.

Look for improvement opportunities

If a part of your daily work process is broken or weak, who is responsible to fix it? Your manager? Yes, they are probably responsible for it, but if you wait for them, get comfortable. These broken processes are like gold nuggets for career advancement. You get the benefit of fixing them and the opportunity to demonstrate your problem-solving skills!

More than anything else, this is a career maker. I can give you countless examples. When a process can be improved, improve it!

Jack recognized that using a printer and paper order tickets to distribute work among 50 team members may not be the best way. There was actually a guy whose job was to grab piles of tickets and distribute them to the appropriate team for execution. At the end of the day, the tickets all had to be re-collected and reconciled to ensure all of the work was complete.

Jack recognized that there was a better way. He approached his manager and asked if he could spend an hour each day for a week on a proposal that could improve things. The manager agreed, and a week later, Jack scheduled some time to review his document.

The manager was very impressed with Jack's plan to create a computer application that made each ticket a line item, with the ability to distribute, track completion and audit right in the application. It even allowed for electronic reconciliation.

This project was bigger than Jack could execute himself, but a month later, he was assigned to be on the project team.

As Jack worked through this project, he suddenly had

exposure to the IT and decision making, and almost daily interaction with more senior management. This experience and interaction is simply irreplaceable when working to advance a corporate career.

Ask for more responsibility

This is one of the most simple, and underused techniques in the corporate world. A fundamental shortcoming of most managers is that they don't harness the potential of their employees. How do you make that work for you? Ask for more responsibility. That's it. Just ask.

This does two things. First, it puts you in your managers head in a positive way. You think you can take on more, and this will influence your manager. Second, you will get more responsibility! There is a huge amount that can be accomplished by just asking.

I can hear some of you saying "Wait, wait, wait...Why would I want more responsibility if I don't get a raise or a promotion?"

The answer is that the responsibility will lead to a promotion. With more responsibilities, you become more well-rounded and more pivotal to your operation. Along with other techniques in this book, this will naturally lead to a promotion and more money. And later I will give some more pointers on how to make sure that happens.

Practice coordination and administrative management skills

So, you've found yourself a job with a solid company, and are working hard to improve yourself. You've managed to gather new responsibilities and have even contributed to an enhancement project. You are probably becoming somewhat of a subject matter expert on your team, and other team members may even come to you for advice. At this point, the next logical progression is to a supervisory/lead/manager position.

Some companies (even good ones) just promote the best subject matter expert (SME) as a matter of course. That is NOT a good thing, for you or for them in most cases. Management is a difficult responsibility, and there are far more bad managers than good ones. Other companies take a more structured approach and evaluate if the SME has the requisite skills, aptitude and potential for a management role.

There are plenty of good management books out there, and I can even recommend a few, but the best thing you can do is get some experience.

Sounds like a chicken or the egg scenario, right? "How can I get management experience if I can't get a job as a manager?"

The answer is to take on lead positions on a smaller scale. Lead a project, take over coordination of a particular task, coordinate an event. Get yourself experience in planning, executing, asking people to do things, and taking ownership of final delivery.

An example, your company asks for volunteers to work on a Saturday to catch up with the backlog of work in counting widgets. I hear an opportunity.

Ask your manager if you can "help" coordinate. Ask broad questions about what the goal of the weekend work is. How much work is needed, what a successful day would look like.

Then figure out how many people are needed, find volunteers, create a schedule, phone list and propose what you think makes sense for divvying up the work.

Saturday rolls around, you have everyone there on time, on task and ready to work. Ask the manager if there is some budget for bagels or lunch, and coordinate that too. If you can, float around and ask if people have questions, and get them answers. Keep track of things, write it down and review as needed.

On a small scale, you now have some management experience. It's going to take more, but coordinating things like this will help you build the skills and experience to make you a shoo-in the next time a management opportunity opens up.

Participate in and eventually lead a project

We touched on this a bit in the last section. Working on, and eventually leading a project is a great career builder. In fact, it can accomplish almost every activity we've discussed thus far. Learning – check. Improvement opportunities – check. More responsibility – check. Coordination and management skills – check.

Working on a project is one of the best things an ambitious person can do. Just make sure, as in all things, you are working hard at it and not taking shortcuts. Be sure to use these opportunities to your full advantage – be proactive.

One of the best examples of someone getting ahead through a project I can think of is a staff member of mine named Jessica.

Jessica was brand new to our company, just a few months out of college. She was sharp and was coming up to speed on her daily responsibilities.

Our company was just launching an enormous project with a new system to support a very popular new business. We had a good amount of funding, but we were short on experienced people. We had to make a tough decision and decided to staff the business side (as opposed to technology) of the project with 4 new employees. Jessica and a guy named Peter were the most experienced, with a combined one year of experience between them. The other two, Kristen and Paul, were pretty much brand new. The group was quickly given the moniker "Green Beans".

This project spanned several teams across the country and had plenty of varying opinions on how every decision should be made. In short, there were more opinions floating around than people who were ready to roll up their sleeves and get things done.

Jessica and Paul immediately got themselves involved. They participated in discussions, rather than just listening. They offered to "run with" things and took ownership of others. In a very short time, they were an integral part of the team. We found ourselves reducing their day to day responsibilities doing data entry and giving them more time to focus on the project.

Kristen and Paul were also busy on the project but kept to themselves and only took responsibilities when asked. They did fine, and just being on the project helped their careers. Peter wound up using his new experience to move to a new company with more responsibility. But it was really Jessica who stepped up and was eventually the main representative of our team to the project.

As the project moved from design, to build, to implementation and eventually to daily use, Jessica found herself the biggest SME in the company on using the new platform. Considering the global scale of this tool, that was quite an accomplishment, especially now that she hit her 3rd anniversary with the company!

During that time, she was promoted twice and was given several awards and bonuses. After a few more months, she moved to a team supporting a new client, and in less than four years was promoted to Officer. Guess how many digits are in her annual salary?

Stay up to date on industry trends and initiatives.

This is an area where you may be able to outperform your managers. Many people get bogged down in the day-to-day affairs of their job and fail to keep an eye on where the industry is going.

Staying up to date on things can really accelerate a

career. There are usually websites, magazines and regular conferences for just about any industry. Get on distribution lists, dial in to the conference calls, read the magazines. Follow your company in the paper if it is large enough, and keep an eye on your competitors, too.

This will be enormously helpful to you understanding the bigger picture of your industry. It will also be a perfect launch pad for an educational conversation with one of your managers. "Stephanie – do you have a few minutes to help me understand what is happening with the new credit card regulations in congress? It seems like that may have an impact on us?"

Suddenly you are getting one on one training with a manager and are sending your career-stock soaring for demonstrating that you see the bigger picture.

Another example, from more of a marketing perspective. Senior Managers often pass an employee, and recognize him based on who he works for, and what that team does. They sometimes don't have much to talk about, so they revert to asking about some new industry initiative. You should be able to respond intelligently!

Bob sees you in in the kitchen, knows you work for Stephanie in Customer Service for the credit card team. Bob doesn't have much in the way of social skills, so he just says, "Looks like some changes on the way for you guys, eh?"

When you respond back with a quick but intelligent view on how it will impact you in six months, you are suddenly the expert on the topic in Bob's eyes. Be ready for a speakerphone call from Bob when he has a question regarding the topic. You'll be prepared, right?

Oh, and when Stephanie puts your name forward for Senior Analyst, Bob will say, "Oh, definitely, they really know their stuff."

Learn how IT projects are initiated, managed and implemented.

Most companies are spending money to improve their technology. It can create huge efficiencies, and really improve the final product or service they are offering. If your company uses any proprietary applications. (i.e. designed and built by your firm, rather than a vendor application.), you most likely have in-house development available.

As a result, knowing the technology process for projects large and small can be hugely beneficial. Most companies will have a process to initiate an IT project. In some cases, it will be as easy as submitting a short web form. Others will have documents that require some degree of detail and various levels of signatures or approvals.

Learn the process and ask more experienced colleagues for tips on getting a project off the ground and delivered successfully. At a minimum, start with a general goal statement – a paragraph or so. Identify a project champion – a manager senior enough to help push the project. I recommend creating a document that outlines complete business requirements, and meeting with IT regularly as the project progresses. Documentation is very important as misunderstandings will undoubtedly occur at times. Be sure to include pertinent dates and revise them as necessary.

 Most likely, the requirements will be refined as you and your IT colleagues work through the solution. Regular meetings will help to work through any issues or discrepancies. Document the outcome of each meeting.

Most firms will have a "beta", "test", or "UAT" environment where the code can be evaluated before being released into the "real world". This allows you to thoroughly test that any code changes you introduce are working.

Early on in the project, create a test plan. Create

multiple scenarios to test that the changes you defined all work as expected. You should have expected results, so that each scenario has a pass/fail. Avoid just having a look and saying, "Seems like it's good.".

Additionally, your test plan should have extensive "regression" scenarios. This tests that everything else you didn't want to change still works properly. These can be re-used for future code releases (combined with scenarios to test the new code – you want to make sure that doesn't break in the future!)

Defining, refining and testing the changes are all obviously important, but be sure that communication is done properly as well. Your changes will impact your team, so they should obviously be in the loop. They'll probably require some training sessions (management experience opportunity) and can probably help with ideas. But be sure to think of other teams as well. A good IT project will have an impact analysis – formal or informal – where all downstream impacts are evaluated. Who else does this project impact inside the company? How about outside? Be sure to communicate early and often to ensure there are no last-minute obstructions to delivering successfully.

Once the project is complete and implemented, be sure to make note as an accomplishment for later (your annual review/self-evaluation, your resume, etc.). It can also be beneficial to send a well-crafted email summarizing the changes and the value created that you can share with your managers. (Don't forget marketing! We'll move on to that next.)

Chapter 5: Market Yourself

This is crucially important. While the true reasons for being promoted lie within the last section, this one is the key to ensuring you get what you deserve. In our football analogy, this is doing the post-game interview patiently and modestly and building up that fan base.

Ask for more responsibility

Wait a second, we already went over this one. You're right, we did, but that was from the perspective of improving yourself. Now we'll look at it from a different perspective – marketing. When you ask the right person for more responsibility, you send a very positive message. Think of one of the senior managers in your group – someone who has maybe 50 people reporting in to them. They may be a Vice President or a Managing Director or something similar.

They are often at the level where they know everyone, and what their general role is, but don't necessarily know about each individuals' skills or performance. Every once in a while, say every six months or so, ask for 15 minutes of their time. Schedule it and be formal about it, respecting the fact that they are probably quite busy.

When you sit down with them, thank them for their

time, and tell them about the positive experiences you are having in your current role. Let them know that you have a strong career path in mind, and that you are always looking for ways to improve yourself and learn. At that point, ask.

"I am hoping you could keep your eyes open for some opportunities for me to take on more responsibilities to help with my career growth."

This will do many things to help you on your way. You've just got them thinking about ways you can contribute more. You are now on their list of potential young stars. You've demonstrated your professionalism and positive attitude. And finally, you've made it clear to a senior manager that you have a career in mind, and that they need to take that into consideration to keep you happy. (Don't go overboard with this one, see Chapter 6...)

Cultivate perception
This concept is pretty straightforward. Your goal here is to always portray yourself in a positive light. Act professionally. Be polite and humble. Demonstrate your worth. Do more than is asked. Generally make every product and situation you are involved in a positive one. Perception is hugely important.

Cultivate relationships inside and outside the company

Relationships are extremely important in business. Now, I am not one of those people who believe that half of business is conducted on the golf course. Not in the corporate world, anyway. But having strong relationships is always a good thing. You never know who may send an email with lavish praise to your bosses or who may wind up BEING your boss someday.

Be sure that you are trying to make a good first impression at every impression. Jane down in accounting, Frank at the new client. Tony's assistant. Treat them all with respect and give them the high-level of professionalism that you'd give to a senior manager or an important client.

Too many times to count, I've gotten a glowing email from an industry contact that dealt with one of my staff and had a positive experience. These are real eye-openers and provide ammunition in your promotion gun. Some managers don't trust their own judgment completely, but if Dan at GE mentioned that someone is really a star, they will believe and they will tell others about it, too.

Express opinions, WITHOUT complaining
Top employees have opinions, and when the time is right, they share them.
"We should be keeping an eye on the developments

with the new widget, so we aren't caught on our heels.", or, "I think we need to do some training sessions on email etiquette."
There will be positives and negatives about every job. You need to be able to discuss both without seeming like you are a complainer. Problems always exist, and they need to be addressed. A team meeting is a good way to address these things, constructively. Always present a solution with the problem. "I'd like to help find some online guidelines for email etiquette."

ALWAYS apply for an opening at the next level
First of all, this can never hurt. If nothing else, it reminds your managers that you are looking for advancement. I have actually surprised myself in the past by getting promotions that I knew I was qualified for but didn't think others knew.

So, if you are a Junior Analyst in accounting, and a Senior Analyst position is available in credit, go for it. But one word of very important caution. Speak to YOUR manager about it first. Many companies have a rule about this, but it ALWAYS makes sense. You can risk alienating your manager if you don't discuss it with them. Be sure to outline that you are not looking to move out of their group, but that you have to consider your career progression, and this makes sense. Either you get it and you get a more senior position, or you don't, and your manager knows you are after that promotion.

Develop your 2 up relationships

A simple fact about promotions – they need a number of layers of approval. Usually it's initiated by your manager, and then approved by their manager or potentially a few layers up. That person at the higher level needs to know who you are. It's even better if they know a lot about you and have a positive impression of you and your work.

So, get to know them. Don't kiss ass, just be friendly and don't be shy about small talk, etc. Following the other tips in this book will go a long way to making a positive impact.

Express interest in management

Some corporate positions have a great job track where you can work individually, but there are plenty more where the only way up after Senior Associate or Specialist is to a manager role. There are almost always more opportunities for advancement in a management track. There just aren't usually as many individual contributor roles at high (paying) levels.

If you express your interest in management, again, it puts it in the mind of your manager, and it makes them comfortable that an investment in developing you will pay off in the long term.

Schedule semi-annual 1 on 1's with your managers,

outside of formal review time

Are you sensing a theme yet? A key point of marketing yourself is keeping you in the heads of the people who control promotions and compensation. Ask your manager for 30 minutes every six months or so. Ask them for feedback on the direction of the organization and if there are things you can do to make yourself more valuable.

Feedback is always good, even when it is negative. It tells you where to improve. But more likely, you'll get positive feedback, and reinforce a strong image in the mind of your manager.

This is a good opportunity to ask about some of the other things we've discussed, such as project opportunities or a management track. It's also a good time to take care of the next point.

ASK how to get your top review rating, 3 months before the review

First of all, this is a winner's question. I've only had a few people do it to me, but it is almost always a top performer. Doing it 3 months in advance gives you an opportunity to tick boxes – to do all the things suggested.

Maybe even more importantly, it sets a tone with your manager that they will have to explain why they DIDN'T give you the top rating. Believe me, if you are a top performer, ask this question, and perform based on the feedback, you will put yourself in a good position. That top review rating is often tied to a formula for calculating your annual raise and bonus. The higher the rating, the bigger the money. One of the most simple but effective techniques, but you need to be a top performer to pull this one off.

Don't be a kiss ass. Do keep yourself noticed.
Don't overdo it. Even mediocre managers can tell when someone is kissing up. You need to be sure that everything you do is truly to add value or to keep yourself appropriately on the minds of your managers. But don't resort to things like complimenting a tie or bringing coffee unsolicited. Use a rule – if you would say it to the security guard, you can say it to your manager. If you are saying it because it is your manager, keep quiet!

You'll alienate yourself from both your manager and your team. That will not be a good thing.

Chapter 6: Forget Yourself

Ever hear an athlete say, "I'm just glad the team was able to put another in the win column."? With some guys, you believe it. With others, you think his agent is feeding him a line. To reach Salarytopia, you need to be the guy who believes it. Your success will come only when the greater organization is successful, IT IS NOT ALL ABOUT YOU.

Be a team-player

I want to be clear about this. The real way to large salaries is by being a valuable asset to your organization. Failure to work effectively with your team will doom you to small paychecks forever. Do not try to get ahead by stepping on others on the way up. Despite Hollywood's attempts to show otherwise, it's not a "Me or Him" situation in most companies.

You need to be able to participate in team settings in all roles – from the low end of the totem pole, just doing grunt work, to being a top contributor who takes on the complex assignments, to the leader who coordinates it all.

Be valuable and be supportive, even if the team isn't top notch or the leader is struggling. Do what you can to keep things on track without blowing up the group dynamic. If you need to criticize something or suggest a change to the leader, do it in private and be sure it is a suggestion, not a veiled command.

"I think it may work to our advantage to meet twice a week without the client to better prepare. What do you think?"

Working well with a team is one of the most important skills to have and you need to consistently demonstrate that. Believe me, if you are not able to work in a team environment, corporate America is not a place to try to grow your career.

Work late/long/weekends when asked, without complaining!
I know it isn't fun or easy to work hard for long hours and very little free time, especially when you are doing it on your entry-level salary. But you need to do it anyway.

It's not enough to be a hard worker. There are plenty of those. You need to combine it with value and skill, but just as importantly, humility. Putting in your time works. You may be used to immediate gratification from school, your parents, etc., but that doesn't usually happen in the corporate world. It's run by consensus and committees. Meaning it takes time. A promotion is often based on performance from several months or a year before!

Take orders without questioning.
This doesn't mean don't ask clarifying questions to ensure you understand the request. This means don't use questions (or comments) to thinly veil contempt for the request. "Why do we have to do this?", is not a good thing.

Remember, this corporation doesn't exist for your advancement. It exists for commercial reasons and is an entity much greater than you. Do what is asked of you and do it well. Gratification comes later.

Say please and thanks.
Very simple, but be polite to everyone. This applies in life in general, but it's vitally important in business. Relationships help you advance.

Be dependable.
If you say you will do it, do it. Meet deadlines. Deliver more than was asked. Remember to do it, even if your boss forgets that he wanted it.

Consider an example, where a manager, Amy, asked an associate, Jim, on another team to forward her an email so she could familiarize herself with it before a client meeting. No problem said Jim. I'll send it right away. He then goes to lunch and forgets all about it.

Amy is unprepared for the meeting and it doesn't go well. Amy mentions it to Jim's boss and his 2-up. Not good.

Later, the Amy is on the committee deciding promotions. I think you can see where this went.

If you aren't dependable, even in the small things, you won't get promotions.

Chapter 7: Check Yourself

This is the hot shot wide receiver saying he doesn't get the ball thrown his way enough, and then getting cut. This is the primadonna cornerback who won't play the run, so he gets put on the bench. This is the Heisman Trophy winner who doesn't get drafted because of his attitude.

This chapter is the most important with regards to those of you who are just joining the workforce or recent grads. I hate to be stereotypical, but it does seem to be a generational thing. You and your contemporaries seem to think the world revolves around you and that you are owed something. You have a sense of entitlement that says the company owes me this or the government owes me that. Well, guess what? They don't.

There are plenty of people around who will deserve a job by earning it every hour of every day. They will be happy to have employment and will recognize that their company really offers them quite an opportunity, and that an opportunity is something that isn't always going to be around.

You can be fired. You may not be able to find another job. Your parents may not be able to support you at 25. You may run out of unemployment. There are CONSEQUENCES to your actions.

I belabor these points because it really seems at times that the latest generation of employees don't seem to get it. I've seen someone say, "You can't do that!", after being fired. Too late. They already did, and your dad and your lawyer can't do anything about it.

So, the good news is, if you actually approach things the right way, and look at your role with some humility and appreciation, you can take advantage of the fact that your peers mostly don't get it.

Be accountable for your own actions.
Do not blame the situation, or the client, or the weather or your car or the traffic. You messed it up, you were late, you got it wrong, etc. Everyone makes mistakes, but you need to own up to it, and stop trying to blame it on your "Computer Disability".

I believe it was Ronald Reagan who once said, *"We must reject the idea that every time a law's broken, society is guilty rather than the lawbreaker. It is time to restore the American precept that each individual is accountable for his actions."*

Be grateful (or at least seem grateful)
Are we clear here? Getting pissed off and complaining when you have to work some overtime is the wrong attitude. Period. There are plenty of people who are dying to pick up enough hours to get their kids some new school clothes, or finally pick up some new tires.

Your job is not owed to you. There are more people out of work now than any time in the last 80 years. You should be grateful for the job, even if you worked your tail off to get it.

Express Opinions *WITHOUT Complaining* 2
Another interesting one. We already covered this in chapter 5. Well, here I want to reiterate - WITHOUT complaining. Yes, you are smart. Yes, hopefully you will have your boss' job one day. But today you don't, and if you are a complainer, you never will, no matter how good and smart you are.

If you need to chip in somewhere that you should probably leave alone, you need to do it in a constructive manner. Schedule some time. Don't be directly critical. Offer to help explore some of the issues. Be diplomatic. And for god sakes, don't complain.

Work late/long/weekends when asked, *without complaining* 2
Are you seeing a pattern here? Good. Enough said.

Remember, you aren't entitled to this job. Or any job. Or really anything at all!

Now, this chapter is fairly short and to the point. It has less direct actions to take and is more about what NOT to do. But notice, it is one of the four pillars, and it has its own chapter. That is because it is VITAL.

You need to get it through your head that you could be on the street someday. You may not be rich. You may not have it better than your parents did.

You can be rich. You can make a lot of money quickly, but you need to take the right steps AND have the right attitude. You need to check yourself.

Conclusion

There's nothing outrageous or earth-shattering here, right? The thing is, most people need to focus more on self-awareness. They may not know what they are doing (or not doing). As I said, follow these guidelines, and you can be earning six figures in just a few years. I've seen it work, and not just once or twice.

Let me reiterate:
This is real advice, from someone who has done it and has shepherded people through it. It is not a get rich quick plan. This book has given you real tools. It is not easy. But it is straightforward. And you can do it. You can reach Salarytopia.

Good luck!